Behind the Scenes

FILM

SARAH MEDINA

First published in 2009 by Wayland

Wayland
338 Euston Road
London NW1 3BH

Wayland Australia
Level 17/ 207 Kent Street
Sydney NSW 2000

Editor: Nicola Edwards
Design manager: Paul Cherrill
Designer: Rita Storey

British Library Cataloguing in Publication Data

Medina, Sarah, 1960-
Film. - (Behind the scenes)
1. Motion pictures - Vocational guidance -
Juvenile literature 2. Motion picture industry - Vocational guidance -
Juvenile literature
I. Title
791.4'0293

ISBN: 978 0 7502 5889 0

The author and publisher would like to thank the following for permission to reproduce the
following photographs and quotations in this book:
© Bob Turner/Alamy p4, © Stuart Kelly/Alamy p5, © Martin Thomas Photography/Alamy p6
© Richard Levine/Alamy p7,© Geraint Lewis/Alamy p8, © Pictorial Press Ltd/Alamy p10,
© brimo/Alamy p11, © *The Guardian* p12, © Keith Morris/Alamy p13, © Shaun Higson
colour/Alamy p24,© Peter Titmuss/Alamy p25, © Steven May/Alamy p27, © Marwood
Jenkins/Alamy p29; Bobby Bank/Wirelmage/Getty Images p15, Robert Patterson/Getty Images
p16, Indranil Mukherjee/AFP/Getty Images p20, Phil Dent/Redferns p21, Frantzesco
Kangaris/AFP/Getty Images p23; istock pp 1, 2, 9, 12, 14, 18, 19, 22, 26, 28 and 29.
Cover image James Devaney/Wirelmage/Getty Images

Printed in China

Wayland is a division of Hachette Children's Books,
an Hachette UK company.
www.hachette.co.uk

Contents

Introduction to film

It is impossible to imagine a world without film. Since the first silent films of the early 20th century, film has entertained, informed and educated millions of people around the world. People traditionally watch films in public places, usually at the cinema, or in the privacy of their home, on TV and DVD. Nowadays, films can be downloaded onto computers and mobile media players, too – and even onto some mobile phones.

Different types of film

Feature films last between about 90 and 200 minutes. Many feature films are made to be shown in cinemas; they are then released onto DVD and, later, shown on TV.

Some feature films, however, are direct-to-DVD, which means that they are not intended to be viewed on the big screen. TV films are made especially for viewing on a television. TV and direct-to-DVD films are often made with much smaller budgets than the big cinema releases.

← Cinema-goers at the Odeon Leicester Square in central London. Film has remained as popular as ever in its longer than 100-year history.

Something for everyone

Film genres are so varied that there are films to appeal to everyone, whatever their age or interests. Action and adventure films are exciting, with big-budget effects and exotic locations. Drama films are normally serious stories, usually with highly developed characters and plots. Horror and science fiction films are tense and often frightening to watch.

Comedy films, from spoofs, such as *Airplane!*, to romantic comedies, such as *Hitch*, all are designed to amuse and make people laugh. Musicals use songs and dance to entertain. Children's and family films are light and entertaining. Animated films, such as the *Shrek* series, use special techniques, such as CGI (computer-generated imagery), to create stories. Actors are used to provide the characters' voices.

About this book

This book gives an overview of the film industry, and the key jobs within it. It includes first-hand accounts of people working in film, and it will help you to work out whether a career in film is for you.

Any questions

Where are films made?

Most people have heard of Hollywood, which is the hub of film-making in the United States. Other important film-making centres are India and China. The British film industry is much smaller, but it is strong and has enjoyed lots of international success over many years.

Working in film

It takes a lot of different people – and many different skills – to make a film. This means that the film industry has a wide range of job opportunities. The key areas in film are development, production, post-production, distribution and exhibition. Film also offers job opportunities in other areas, including transport, catering, accounts and human resources (HR). Within each of these areas, there is plenty of scope for career progression as people gain experience.

Development

Development is the earliest stage of film-making. It is all about planning a film: coming up with and then developing ideas, and obtaining funding so that the project can go ahead. Work in this area includes writing screenplays, preparing budgets and schedules, and getting a film crew together.

Production

Production is all about setting up and shooting the film, scene by scene. There are many different elements involved in film production, from designing and creating sets

↓ *Actors such as Uma Thurman, seen here on a film set in California, USA, know that working in film is hard work and very competitive. It is also fast-moving and highly creative.*

and costumes, to technical operations such as cameras, sound and lighting, to directing the whole process.

effects and graphics are added, as well as different sounds, such as speech, music and sound effects.

Post-production

Post-production is the area that brings everything together into a finished product after filming. During post-production, parts of a film may be cut and other parts pieced together. Visual

Distribution

Distribution is all about bringing a finished film in front of an audience. Some distribution staff are responsible for licensing, which means obtaining the right to show a film to an audience. Others are responsible for marketing the film, so that as many people as possible see it.

THINKING AHEAD

Many people want to work in film, especially as actors or directors, because they want to become rich and famous. However, most people in film are not well-known – and most earn an average income, too. It is much better to work in film simply because you are passionate about film-making.

Exhibition

Exhibition staff are responsible for showing films to an audience. This normally happens in cinemas – from large cinema chains to small independent cinemas. Films may also be shown at national or international film festivals and other events.

Development

In film-making, development is the early ideas stage. Ideas for films may be completely new and original, or they may grow out of material that already exists, such as books, plays and TV programmes. Some of the key jobs in development are script developer and screenwriter.

Script developer

Script developers work at the very initial stages of the film-making process. A script developer is responsible for researching new ideas and finding good screenwriters. When a script developer decides to pursue an idea, he or she works closely with the screenwriter as the screenplay progresses.

Sometimes, a script developer helps to raise finance for a film. In the UK, funding may come from a variety of sources, for example: from organizations that finance British film-making, such as the UK Film Council; from broadcasters, such as the BBC; and from production companies involved with the film.

↓ *Many feature films are based on stage plays. Mamma Mia!, which was a huge box-office hit, was based on a musical of the same name.*

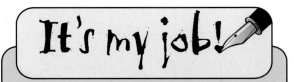

It's my job!

Edward: Script developer in a film production company

"To be good at this job, I need to stay on top of my game. It's easy to find an idea for a film – but much harder to find an idea that will work both creatively and commercially. I need to able to predict future trends and to know how well any given idea will fit into the market."

Screenwriter

Without screenwriters, there would be nothing to film! A screenwriter writes the film's screenplay, which contains all the words that the actors say, as well as instructions for the film shoot.

Often, screenwriters write a treatment before completing a screenplay. A treatment is like a brief sales pitch: a summary of the characters, action and style of the film. Screenwriters may send a treatment to a script developer, director or producer, in the hope that they will want to commission the screenplay.

Sometimes, a screenwriter is approached to write a screenplay for

an idea that already exists. Some films, for example, are based on novels or biographies. On some films, screenwriters may work in a team. Within the team, different writers are responsible for different parts of the screenplay.

THINKING AHEAD

It can take years to complete a screenplay, and many screenplays are never even filmed. To work as a screenwriter, you need to be patient and prepared to work with others on your ideas. You also need to have very thick skin as your work will be scrutinized and criticized from beginning to end!

↑ *Screenwriters must be prepared to rewrite a script – often, several times – in line with the film director's vision.*

Production

Jobs in film production are very varied. Some jobs, such as set designer and make-up and hair designer, are very artistic. Some, such as lighting and camera roles, are highly technical. Others, such as producer, are more managerial. This section looks at some of the key jobs in production.

Director

The director is the person who has overall creative responsibility for the way a film is made. It is the director's interpretation of a screenplay that we see when we go to the cinema, or watch a film on DVD or TV.

THINKING AHEAD

To be a director, you need a visual brain, which can picture how a screenplay will work as moving images and sound. Excellent communication skills are important, too, because this is a job that involves working with – and directing – many different people.

↓ The director Mike Newell oversees the shoot for the film Mona Lisa Smile. The cast and crew all have to listen carefully to his instructions.

During development, directors work with the screenwriter on the development of the screenplay. During production, they work closely with many production staff, discussing ideas and giving instructions so that the film evolves according to their vision. Directors are involved with choosing the cast, crew and filming locations, and with planning the shoot. During post-production, directors work with editors until they are happy with the final version of the film.

Assistant directors

A director's job is a huge one, and assistant directors (known as ADs) are there to help with different aspects of the work. The first AD helps the director to plan the shoot, and then puts together and oversees the filming schedule. The second AD supports the first AD's work. During filming, the second AD manages the call sheet, and makes sure that the main actors are in the right place at the right time. The third AD helps the first and second ADs

in any way that is required; he or she is normally involved with overseeing the extras (who are also known as supporting artists) during a shoot.

Any questions

What is the best entry-level job in film?

The most junior member of a film crew is the runner. A runner's job is to run errands for the cast and crew – anything from photocopying and typing to driving to making cups of tea! Being a runner can be hard work for little pay, but it is a great way to get a start in the industry.

→ *Some production companies offer work experience placements as runners to people who are interested in working in the film industry. Being a runner can be the first step to getting the job you want.*

Producer

A producer is involved with every area of film-making, from development to distribution. It is often a producer who comes up with an initial idea for a film, and then finds the people to make it happen – including the screenwriter and the director. Whereas a director has overall creative responsibility for a film, a producer has more hands-on, practical responsibility for the business side of the film.

The producer is involved with raising finance for a film. The budget for a film can run into millions of pounds – and, during production, the producer is responsible for the film being made within budget. Films may entertain an audience, but they have to make money, too. To ensure the greatest profit, the producer helps to shape marketing plans and to find distributors for the film.

Any questions?

Is being a producer more about making money than being creative?

Paul Webster is head of film at Shine Pictures in London and has produced such box office successes as *Atonement* and *Pride and Prejudice*. He says of being a film producer: "If you set out to get rich you're 99% doomed to failure, you've got to be driven by a passion..."

→ A producer looks after the financial side of film-making, from raising finance to maximizing profits.

Production manager

Production managers support the work of the producer. They work closely with the whole team to make sure that the production runs smoothly. For example, they work with unit managers to select locations for filming, and they liaise with first ADs to make sure that the filming schedule is kept to.

A production manager's job can often involve a lot of administration and staff management. For example, production managers may write the contracts for the members of the cast and crew, and are involved with decisions regarding their pay and working conditions.

Location manager

Location managers are responsible for finding locations for a film shoot. They have to make sure that the location is suitable and available, and that it is not too expensive to film there. They agree contracts for using different locations, and they are in charge of the location during the shoot.

➡

Location managers have to consider many things before deciding on a location, including accessibility for cast and crew, and vehicles and equipment.

Casting director

A casting director is responsible for finding actors for a film and for agreeing the terms of their contract. They oversee auditions, and they work closely with the director and producer to select the best actors for the different roles. A casting director needs to have a thorough understanding of acting – and a detailed knowledge of which actors there are to choose from.

Actor

An actor's job involves interpreting a screenplay to bring a character in a film to life. Sometimes, an actor does a lot of research to understand and 'get into' a role. Actors always work closely with the director, so they understand his or her vision for the character and for the film as a whole. An actor normally attends a series of meetings and auditions, before being selected for a job.

Stunt performer

A stunt performer usually takes the place of an actor in scenes that contain potentially dangerous action, or when specific skills, such as martial arts, are required. Stunt performers can be seriously injured or even killed, so everyone takes every possible precaution to reduce risk.

← *An actor studies his script as he waits to be called for an audition. Good casting contributes to a film's success, so it is important that the casting director finds actors who are most suitable for a role.*

↑ *A stunt crew films* Spider Man 3 *on location in New York City, USA. Stunt performers are extremely fit and highly trained people.*

Composer

A composer is a person who writes music. In the film industry, a composer writes original music for a film. The composer liaises with the film's director because, to write the best music, it is important to understand the director's creative vision.

Any questions ?

Do actors ever do their own stunts?

Yes, some actors prefer to do their own stunts – or, at least, some of them! Daniel Craig, who starred in the James Bond films *Casino Royale* and *Quantum of Solace*, leapt off high buildings and onto moving vehicles during filming. He says, "I've thrown myself into it because I get a kick out of it... It's much better if I stay involved with the filming as much as possible."

Production designer

An production designer oversees the art department on a film production. He or she works with the director to create the overall visual look of the film, which includes the different locations, sets, props, costumes and make-up. As a starting point, the production designer studies the screenplay in detail. He or she also needs to consider the film's budget, so that the design plans are not too expensive. Once designs have been approved, the production designer provides design sketches to the art director.

Art director

An art director is responsible for bringing a production designer's visual ideas into being. Before filming, the art director oversees a team of people who build the set and decorate it with props. During rehearsals, set designers may make adjustments to the set, if necessary.

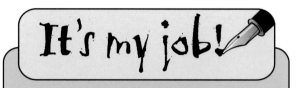

It's my job!

Tony: Art director

"It's great working with the team and seeing different sets taking shape. It can be quite a stressful job, though. For one, I have to keep a close eye on the budget to make sure that we don't overspend. And keeping to schedule is critical – we'd be in big trouble if the sets weren't ready on time. We usually start work months before filming actually begins."

← *The director Peter Jackson is seen here with props from his three* Lord of the Rings *films. Props are an important part of any film set, and help to make the scene look and feel realistic.*

Costume designer

A costume designer is responsible for designing, hiring and adapting costumes for the actors in a film. Depending on the film, they may need to work on period, modern-day or futuristic designs. In order to be accurate, costume designers need to know about the kinds of clothes that people wore at particular times in history. They also need to have a good understanding of each character in the film, so they can get a feel for the clothes the character would wear.

THINKING AHEAD

Costume designers need to be creative, as well as practical. Sometimes, costumes are designed and created from scratch. At other times, costume designers need to be able to make changes to costumes that they have hired for the film.

Make-up and hair designer

Make-up and hair designers design and apply make-up for actors before and during a film shoot. They are also responsible for an actor's hairstyle, which may include designing wigs, hair extensions or bald caps. For some films, make-up and hair designers create prosthetics for effects such as scars, cuts and bruises.

← Actors don't always have to look good! A make-up and hair designer needs to know how to recreate effects such as a black eye accurately.

Director of photography

A director of photography (or DoP) works to make the director's creative vision for a film a reality. Collaboration with the director and the production designer is essential in this job, especially in the planning stages. The DoP liaises closely with the camera and lighting crews, too, to ensure that camera and lighting choices achieve the desired effect.

Camera operator

A camera operator sets up and works the cameras used for shooting different scenes in a film. Working with the DoP, the camera operator decides on the cameras and other equipment, such as cranes and pulleys, and the best camera positions, for each shoot.

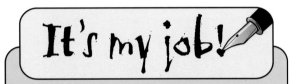

It's my job!

Finn: Director of photography

"At the moment, I'm working on big epic adventure film. My job is creative and technical at the same time. I have to translate creative ideas into a visual reality, by making selecting the best camera angles, lighting effects and so on. Before filming, I work out all the equipment we need for the shoot. Then, when filming starts, I oversee the process to make sure that the right effects are being achieved."

THINKING AHEAD

Camera operators need to have strong technical ability – and a good creative eye so, for example, they can frame a shot in the best possible way. There is a lot happening in a film shoot, and camera operators need to be able to respond quickly to instructions from the director or DoP.

↓ Lighting is a highly technical area, and DoPs need to understand how to create different lighting effects so they can work effectively with camera operators.

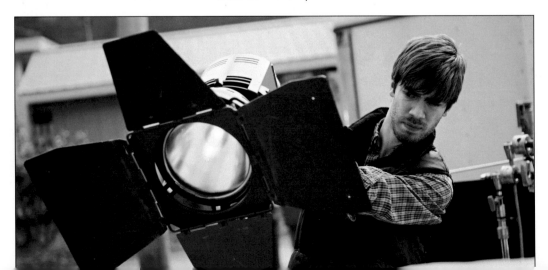

Gaffer

A gaffer oversees a team of electricians, who set up lighting equipment and power supplies for a film shoot. He or she is also responsible for operating and maintaining the lighting and related equipment during production. Health and safety is an important part of a gaffer's job; he or she needs to make sure that all equipment on a film set meets the required standards.

Production sound mixer

A production sound mixer is the person responsible for recording high-quality dialogue during a film shoot. This can be challenging because the conditions on a film set – for example, on a shoot in a tight space, such as in an underground cave – often make it hard to place equipment such as microphones in the best possible place.

During filming, the production sound mixer monitors the sound quality after each take and, if the sound quality is not up-to-scratch, requests a new take. Then the scene has to be filmed again.

← *A gaffer needs to be able to handle the full range of electrical equipment, from cables to generators, as well as managing the team.*

Any questions ?

Where does the term "gaffer" come from?

One explanation given by people in the film industry is that the name comes from the "gaff poles" that lighting technicians used. The poles had hooks on the ends that could move roof panels to let sunlight in when it was needed to light a set.

Post-production

During post-production, all the hard work of planning and filming comes together. This is where the director finds out whether the final film matches his or her original vision! Some of the key jobs in post-production are editor and re-recording mixer.

Editor

An editor puts together the final film that you and I watch at the cinema or at home. Specialist editing equipment enables the editor to combine camera footage, speech, sound effects, music, graphics and visual effects.

↓ *Film editor Deepa Bhati works on Bollywood films. An editor often works alone, but collaboration with the director is essential.*

During a shoot, much more material is filmed than is actually needed to make a film of the correct length. Every piece of footage that is filmed is stored separately and has its own number. During editing, editors select the very best footage for each scene. Using computer software, they join together the different pieces of footage to form a sequence. All the sequences are then combined, and sound, music and visual effects added in, to make the final film.

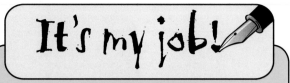

Marian: Editor

"I work on a freelance basis, and I have worked on different types of films. Right now, I'm working on a horror film. Although a lot of what I do happens during post-production, I am involved with the film way before then. Before filming, I can give ideas to the director about how to get the best out of the screenplay. During filming, I check each day's shoot to make sure that the story is coming together, and that technical requirements are met. It's a full-on job, combining creativity and technical skills – and I love it!"

→

Director Mel Gibson sits at the mixing desk in a recording studio as he and his colleagues listen to the soundtrack of his film Braveheart.

THINKING AHEAD

Re-recording mixers need to be able to concentrate for long periods. A good ear is vital, because they need to be able to hear subtle sounds and effects. They need technical ability, too, to handle the range of complex equipment required to do their job.

Re-recording mixer

A re-recording mixer brings together the all the recorded dialogue, music and sound effects in a film. He or she may add extra sound effects in the post-production stage, too. Re-recording mixers work in sound-proofed studios or editing suites. They sometimes work with other post-production staff, such as sound editors, to make sure that the level of sound is consistent and that the sound quality is high.

21

Distribution

Without distribution, no one would get to see a finished film! This part of the film industry is, for this reason, just as important as all the others. Films are made to make a profit – and it is through distribution deals that these profits can be made. Some of the key jobs in distribution are distributor, and marketing and publicity manager.

Distributor

A distributor is responsible for obtaining the legal right to show a film to an audience, for example, in the cinema, on DVD or on TV.

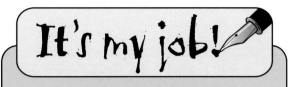

It's my job!

Geoff: Distributor

"Being a distributor is all about maximising profits for the film distribution company I work for. To be successful at my job, I need to know the film market backwards! For example, I know that some cinemas will do better than others at getting people in to watch a particular film, maybe, by offering special promotions – and these are the cinemas I need to work with. It can be challenging, but it is satisfying knowing that you have made the best deal you can."

↓ *Distributors need to weigh up the costs of promoting a film with the profits that can be made from the licensing deal.*

This is known as licensing. There are two types of licensing: international, which means that a film can be shown around the world; and local, which means that the distributor can only release the film in one country.

After obtaining the required licence, distributors are then responsible for launching the film, perhaps by means of a film premiere. The idea is to create as much interest in the film as possible, so that as many people as possible pay to watch it, thereby increasing the profit made by the film.

Marketing and publicity manager

A marketing and publicity manager is responsible for putting together a marketing campaign for a film. The purpose of the marketing campaign is to bring the film to the attention of as wide an audience as possible. For major feature films, marketing campaigns can be very expensive, but the idea is that expenditure is rewarded with big audiences, which means big profits.

↓ *A model wears a dress made of shopping bags to welcome guests to the London premiere of the film Confessions of a* Shopaholic *in 2009. Marketing and publicity is all about making a film a 'must-see' film of the moment!*

Other jobs in film

Many of the jobs in film are specialized. However, more general job opportunities are available in the film industry, too. These include jobs in catering, transport, accounts, human resources (usually called HR), and legal departments. Whatever their role, people enjoy having the chance to be part of the film industry.

Catering

Everyone needs to eat – and the cast and crew on film sets are no exception! Film shoots can be very long, and three meals a day – breakfast, lunch and dinner – are often provided by a specialist catering company, which is hired by a production manager. Food is carried and prepared in, and served

It's my job!

Veronica: Location chef

"I work as part of the catering crew preparing food on big film productions. As a location chef, I come up with menu ideas, which have to be approved by my manager. I then work with the other catering staff to prepare and serve the meals from our massive truck. We work long, hard days and it can be really stressful. Sometimes, I've had to start work at three o'clock in the morning! But I work with a great bunch of people in this mobile kitchen, and I enjoy making sure that everyone is fed and watered. You get to meet some really cool people, too."

← Catering staff work at the hub of film making. Preparing food on location is both challenging and rewarding.

from, huge catering vehicles by catering crew. Tea and coffee are also provided throughout the day.

Transport

Transport staff are responsible for making sure that the cast and crew on a film production get to the location of the film shoot. They also transport important equipment, such as cameras and props for a film set.

Transport is more complicated – and essential – than it sounds. If someone or something is missing from a shoot, it can be a very expensive mistake. Films are usually shot in multiple locations, often in different countries. Travel arrangements can be tricky, and permits may need to be obtained. Transport staff need to be highly organized and on the ball.

On big film shoots, a transport coordinator is responsible for overseeing all of the transport requirements. A transport manager oversees the large vehicles needed for production, such as, mobile make-up and costume units. A number of different drivers are also needed.

Any questions?

How do I get into film?

Jobs in film are in high demand. Many people who work in film need a university degree to get a foot in the door. However, there are other ways in to the industry. Doing work experience, for example, as a runner (see page 11), gives you experience and contacts that can lead to the job you really want.

↓ *Vast amounts of equipment need to be moved around for different shoots. Without transport staff, filming would come to a standstill.*

Accounts

Accounts staff are responsible for dealing with financial matters, such as paying invoices, for hiring the costumes or props for a shoot, for example; and receiving payments, for instance, from broadcasters from other countries who buy a particular programme. The accounts department is also responsible for staff pay, tax and pensions.

Human Resources

HR is all about human beings – the people who work for a film production company. HR staff are involved with all issues relating to staff employment, from hiring to firing. They can also advise employees who have work-related problems.

Legal

Legal staff are normally qualified lawyers, who can advise film industry staff on a range of issues. For example, they may help HR staff with queries about employment law, or they may advise a director about whether information to be included in a film is libellous. Legal staff may also draw up contracts for people who are involved on a film, many of whom work on a freelance basis.

↓ *Office-based work, such as accounting, HR and legal, is an essential part of the film industry.*

Film and you

Film is an exciting and creative industry. Being part of the film industry can give people a real buzz. Watching a film that you have helped to make – and seeing other people enjoy it – at the cinema, or on DVD or TV, is incredibly satisfying.

The flip side is that jobs in film are notoriously difficult to find – and keep. Even when you are experienced and well-established in film, there is little or no job security. Most people who work in film are freelance. Many films fall through because of lack of funding, and so some people rely on work that does not, in the end, materialize.

On the job, the work can be stressful, too. Working hours in the film industry are long, and people often work under a lot of pressure. Conditions, especially on outdoor shoots, may be uncomfortable. The day-to-day reality of working in film may not match up to its glamorous image.

↓ *It is important to weigh up the pros and cons of an area of work – and film is no exception. Only then can you work out if the film industry will suit you.*

If you are interested in working in film, it helps to find out as much as you can about the industry. Reading this book is a good start! You will be able to find out more information from a careers office or library. The further reading list on page 31 will point you in the direction of some useful books and websites.

Think about the kinds of interests you have, and what you are good at. Do these tie in with a particular job or area in film? For example:

- Are you creative and do you love writing? If so, you could consider becoming a screenwriter.

- Are you into fashion – not just what's in right now, but what people have worn over history? In that case, costume design might be your thing.

- Have you got a good ear for sound and music and are you good with technology? If so, you might enjoy having a job as a re-recording mixer.

THINKING AHEAD

Try your hand at making your own short films. You do not need specialist equipment – a simple video recorder will do the trick. There are lots of websites that will help you to get going; see page 31 for ideas. Even though it is only on a small scale, there is no better way to find out about film than by getting on and making one!

↓ *With a video recorder and a computer with basic sound and editing programs, you can gain some valuable film-making experience.*

University students on a media studies course get hands-on experience of shooting a film.

Research the qualities and skills you need to work in the area of film that interests you. For example, to be a film editor, you need to be creative, confident and patient – and you have to be able to concentrate for long periods of time. These are qualities; they are largely to do with your personality. You also need to understand film production and to know how to use specialist film editing equipment. These are skills that can be learned.

If you believe that working in film is for you and that you have what it takes to make a go of it, then research, plan and prepare. It is a competitive world, but it is very rewarding. Do everything you can to achieve your goal. Good luck!

Any questions

How do I improve my chances of working in film?
Work experience is a fantastic way to gain inside knowledge of the film industry. Most work experience is as a runner. Runners may be at the bottom rung of the film ladder, but they meet all sorts of different people – from directors and producers to production crew and actors. If you work hard and make a good impression, these contacts can make all the difference to getting that important first job in film.

Glossary

audition a short performance given by an actor to show his or her suitability for a part in a film

budget money allocated to a project

call sheet a document that gives the detail of what is happening on each day of a shoot, which is used by cast and crew

cast actors and other performers in a film

CEO chief executive officer – the most important position in a company

CGI computer-generated imagery

commission choose someone to do a piece of work, and tell them what is needed

crane a tall metal structure used for lifting and moving heavy equipment

crew the group of people who work together on making a film

design sketch a sketch prepared by production designers, detailing design issues for film sets, such as mood, atmosphere, lighting colours and textures

edit prepare the final cut of a film by deciding what will be included and removing any mistakes

extra a person in a film – often in the background – who does not have a speaking part. Extras are also known as supporting artists

film premiere when a film is shown for the first time to an audience of invited guests

footage piece of film

freelance being self-employed and working for a company on a project by-project basis

funding money given by a government or organization so that a particular film can be made

graphics visual material used as part of a film

libellous containing false information about a person

licensing when a distributor has the legal right to show a film to audiences, either within one country or internationally

prop an object needed for a film set, such as a doctor's stethoscope or a pirate's sword, to make the set seem natural and realistic

prosthetics appliances made of materials such as rubber, plastic or silicone, which are attached to an actor's face or body to change its shape or appearance

pulley a piece of equipment used for moving heavy objects up or down

schedule a list of activities to be completed on a project, with dates by which each activity needs to be completed

screenplay the text for a film, including the actors' words and instructions for filming

set the collection of scenery to be used for a scene in a programme

shoot when a particular scene for a programme is filmed

sound effect a sound other than speech or music, which is added to a film's soundtrack to make it seem more realistic

take the filming of a scene in a film

treatment a short version of a screenplay, with a summary of the main features, such as characters and plot

work experience a short period of time that someone spends working for a film company, often without pay

Further information

The Creative and Media Diploma

The Diploma is a qualification for 14 to 19 year-olds which combines classroom-based study with practical hands-on work experience. It enables you to find out more about the careers you're interested in without having to commit to one of them. Find out more information about the Creative and Media Diploma at:
http://yp.direct.gov.uk/diplomas/ subjects/Creative_Media/index.cfm

Film Qualifications and Training

Most people who work in film go to university from school. Many do an arts, or a film or media studies, degree, but this is not essential for all jobs in film. Opportunities are always available for people who show talent and dedication, even if they have not taken a media-specific course.

Books

People at Work: Creative and Media by Jan Champney (Franklin Watts, 2008)

Getting into Films and Television by Robert Angell (How To Books, 2004)

Creative Careers: Film by Milly Jenkins (Trotman and Company, 2003)

A Career Handbook for TV, Radio, Film, Video and Interactive Media by Shiona Llewellyn and Sue Walker* (A&C Black, second edition, 2003)

Websites

For more information about working in the film industry:
www.skillset.org/film
http://www.skillset.org/film/stories/ (success stories)

This website for young people tells you all about how to make a film:
www.firstlightmovies.com/how_to_ make_a_film/

For information about key production jobs in broadcasting, film and video:
www.prospects.ac.uk/cms/ShowPage /Home_page/Explore_types_of_jobs/ Types_of_Job/p!eipaL?grpno=Y5& state=showgrp

For information about key technical jobs in broadcasting, film and video:
www.prospects.ac.uk/cms/ShowPage /Home_page/Explore_types_of_jobs /Types_of_Job/p!eipaL?grpno=Y4& state=showgrp

For information about training courses in film:
www.britfilms.com/training/

For information about how to get a job in film and television, and examples of how other people got started:
www.film-tv.co.uk/

For general information and advice about careers:
www.connexions-direct.com/ index.cfm?go=Careers

Index

Numbers in **bold** refer to pictures.

Behind the Scenes

Contents of titles in the series:

WAYLAND